Daniel Yiu 4L.

Intermediate 2 | Units 1, 2 & 3
Mathematics

2004 Exam
Paper 1 (Non-Calculator)
Paper 2

2005 Exam
Paper 1 (Non-Calculator)
Paper 2

2006 Exam
Paper 1 (Non-Calculator)
Paper 2

2007 Exam
Paper 1 (Non-Calculator)
Paper 2

2008 Exam
Paper 1 (Non-Calculator)
Paper 2

Leckie×Leckie

© Scottish Qualifications Authority
All rights reserved. Copying prohibited. No part of this publication may be reproduced, stored in a retrieval system, or transmitted in any form or by any means, electronic, mechanical, photocopying, recording or otherwise.

First exam published in 2004.
Published by Leckie & Leckie Ltd, 3rd Floor, 4 Queen Street, Edinburgh EH2 1JE
tel: 0131 220 6831 fax: 0131 225 9987 enquiries@leckieandleckie.co.uk www.leckieandleckie.co.uk

ISBN 978-1-84372-664-7

A CIP Catalogue record for this book is available from the British Library.

Leckie & Leckie is a division of Huveaux plc.

Leckie & Leckie is grateful to the copyright holders, as credited at the back of the book, for permission to use their material.
Every effort has been made to trace the copyright holders and to obtain their permission for the use of copyright material.
Leckie & Leckie will gladly receive information enabling them to rectify any error or omission in subsequent editions.

2004 | Intermediate 2

[BLANK PAGE]

X100/201

NATIONAL
QUALIFICATIONS
2004

FRIDAY, 21 MAY
1.00 PM – 1.45 PM

MATHEMATICS
INTERMEDIATE 2
Units 1, 2 and 3
Paper 1
(Non-calculator)

Read carefully

1 You may **NOT** use a calculator.

2 Full credit will be given only where the solution contains appropriate working.

3 Square-ruled paper is provided.

FORMULAE LIST

The roots of $ax^2 + bx + c = 0$ are $x = \dfrac{-b \pm \sqrt{(b^2 - 4ac)}}{2a}$

Sine rule: $\dfrac{a}{\sin A} = \dfrac{b}{\sin B} = \dfrac{c}{\sin C}$

Cosine rule: $a^2 = b^2 + c^2 - 2bc \cos A$ or $\cos A = \dfrac{b^2 + c^2 - a^2}{2bc}$

Area of a triangle: Area $= \tfrac{1}{2} ab \sin C$

Volume of a sphere: Volume $= \tfrac{4}{3} \pi r^3$

Volume of a cone: Volume $= \tfrac{1}{3} \pi r^2 h$

Volume of a cylinder: Volume $= \pi r^2 h$

Standard deviation: $s = \sqrt{\dfrac{\sum (x - \bar{x})^2}{n-1}} = \sqrt{\dfrac{\sum x^2 - (\sum x)^2 / n}{n-1}}$, where n is the sample size.

ALL questions should be attempted.

Marks

1. In a class test, the following marks were recorded.

    5   9   10   4   5   5   6   10   5   8
    5   7   4   9   7   5   4   6   5   7

   (a) Construct a frequency table for the above data and add a cumulative frequency column.   2

   (b) What is the probability that a student, chosen at random from this class, obtained a mark higher than 7?   1

2.

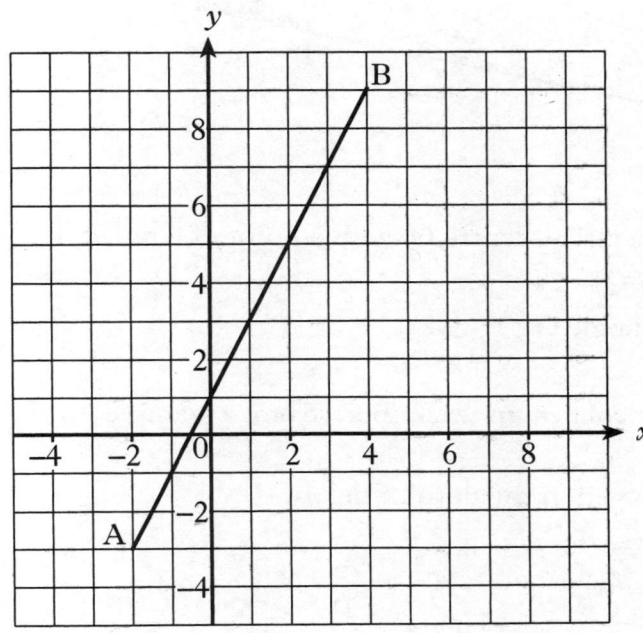

Find the equation of the straight line AB.   3

[Turn over

Marks

3.

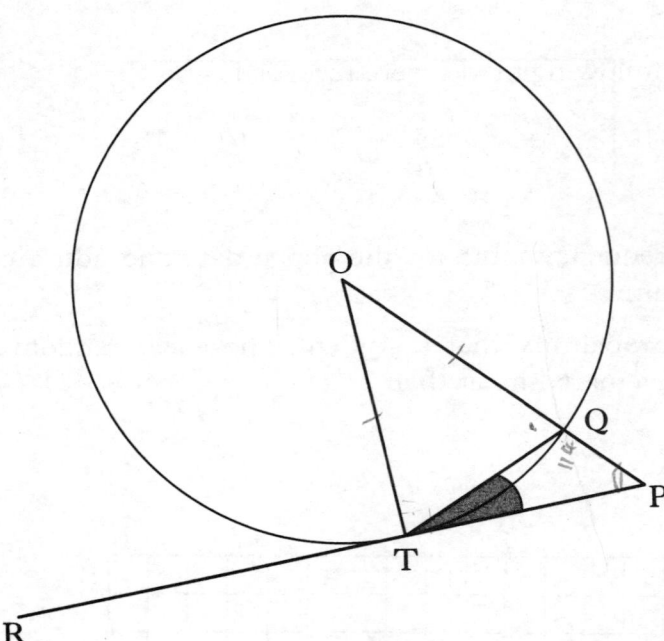

RP is a tangent to the circle, centre O, with a point of contact T.
The shaded angle PTQ = 24°.
Calculate the size of angle OPT.

3

4. The number of chocolates in each box from a sample of 25 boxes was counted.
The results are displayed in the dotplot below.

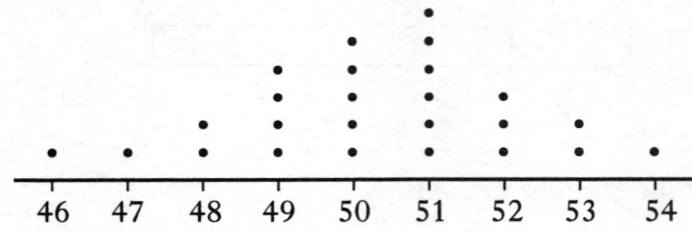

(a) For this sample find:
  (i) the median; **1**
  (ii) the lower quartile; **1**
  (iii) the upper quartile. **1**

(b) Use the data from this sample to construct a boxplot. **2**

(c) In a second sample of boxes, the semi-interquartile range was 1·5.

Make an appropriate comment about the distribution of data in the two samples. **2**

5. William Watson's Fast Foods use a logo based on parts of three identical parabolas.

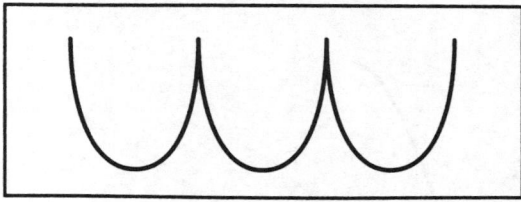

This logo is represented on the diagram below.

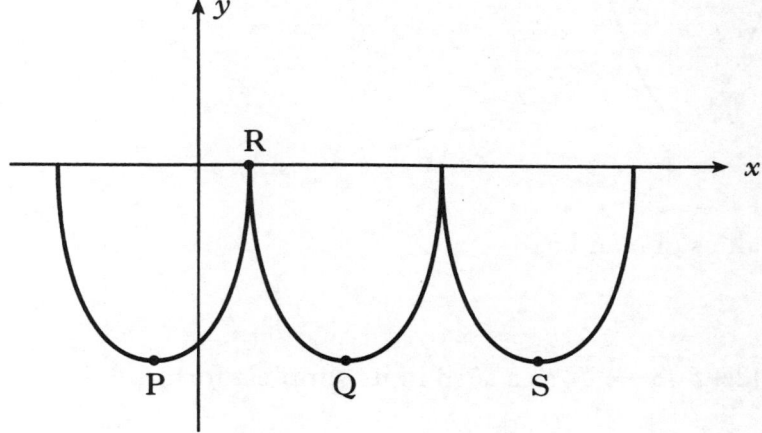

The first parabola has turning point P and equation $y = (x + 2)^2 - 16$.

(a) State the coordinates of P. **2**

(b) If R is the point (2, 0), find the coordinates of Q, the minimum turning point of the second parabola. **1**

(c) Find the equation of the parabola with turning point S. **2**

[Turn over for Question 6 on Page six

6. (a) Part of the graph of $y = b \cos ax°$ is shown in the diagram.

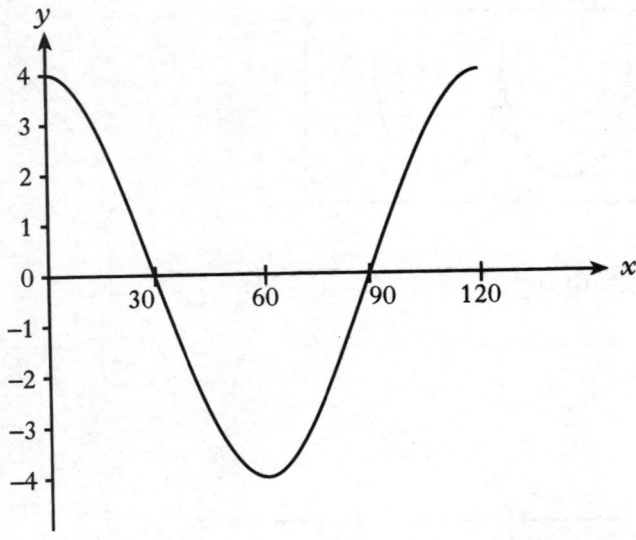

State the values of a and b. **2**

(b) Express $\sqrt{12} + 5\sqrt{3} - \sqrt{27}$ as a surd in its simplest form. **3**

[END OF QUESTION PAPER]

X100/203

NATIONAL
QUALIFICATIONS
2004

FRIDAY, 21 MAY
2.05 PM – 3.35 PM

MATHEMATICS
INTERMEDIATE 2
Units 1, 2 and 3
Paper 2

Read carefully

1 **Calculators may be used in this paper.**

2 Full credit will be given only where the solution contains appropriate working.

3 Square-ruled paper is provided.

FORMULAE LIST

The roots of $ax^2 + bx + c = 0$ are $x = \dfrac{-b \pm \sqrt{(b^2 - 4ac)}}{2a}$

Sine rule: $\dfrac{a}{\sin A} = \dfrac{b}{\sin B} = \dfrac{c}{\sin C}$

Cosine rule: $a^2 = b^2 + c^2 - 2bc \cos A$ or $\cos A = \dfrac{b^2 + c^2 - a^2}{2bc}$

Area of a triangle: Area $= \tfrac{1}{2} ab \sin C$

Volume of a sphere: Volume $= \tfrac{4}{3} \pi r^3$

Volume of a cone: Volume $= \tfrac{1}{3} \pi r^2 h$

Volume of a cylinder: Volume $= \pi r^2 h$

Standard deviation: $s = \sqrt{\dfrac{\sum(x - \bar{x})^2}{n-1}} = \sqrt{\dfrac{\sum x^2 - (\sum x)^2 / n}{n-1}}$, where n is the sample size.

ALL questions should be attempted.

Marks

1. The average Scottish house price is £77 900.

   The average price is expected to rise by 2·5% per month. What will the average Scottish house price be in 3 months?

   Give your answer correct to three significant figures. **3**

2. The heights, in millimetres, of six seedlings are given below.

   $$15 \quad 18 \quad 14 \quad 17 \quad 16 \quad 19$$

   (a) Calculate:
   - (i) the mean; **1**
   - (ii) the standard deviation; **3**

   of these heights.

   Show clearly all your working.

   (b) Later the same six seedlings are measured again.

   Each has grown by 4 millimetres.

   State:
   - (i) the mean; **1**
   - (ii) the standard deviation; **1**

   of the new heights.

3. (a) Multiply out the brackets and collect like terms.

   $$5x + (x - 4)(3x + 1)$$ **3**

   (b) Factorise

   $$3x^2 - 7x + 2.$$ **2**

   [Turn over

Marks

4.

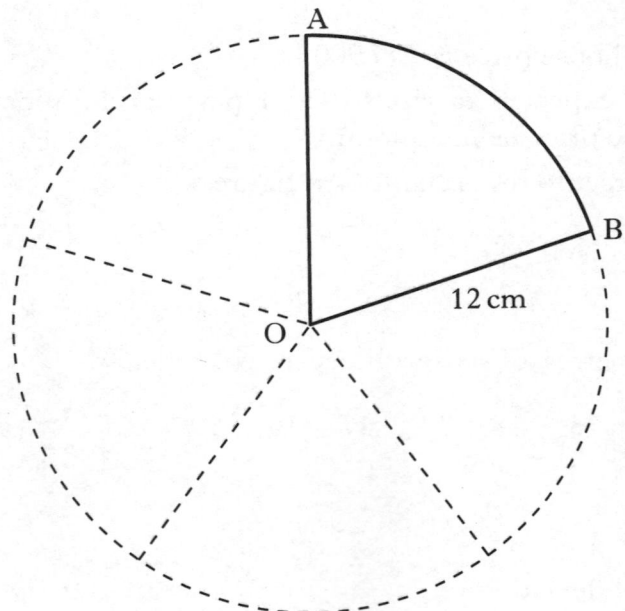

A circle, with centre O and radius 12 centimetres, is cut into 5 equal sectors.
Calculate the perimeter of sector OAB.   3

5. A sports centre charges different entrance fees for adults and children.

(a) One evening 14 adults and 4 children visited the sports centre. The total collected in entrance fees was £55·00.

Let £x be the adult's entrance fee and £y be the child's entrance fee.

Write down an equation in x and y which represents the above condition.   1

(b) The following evening 13 adults and 6 children visited the sports centre. The total collected in entrance fees was £54·50.

Write down a second equation in x and y which represents the above condition.   1

(c) Calculate the entrance fee for an adult and the entrance fee for a child.   4

Marks

6. Solve the equation $2x^2 + 7x - 3 = 0$, giving the roots correct to one decimal place.   4

7. A garden, in the shape of a quadrilateral, is represented in the diagram below.

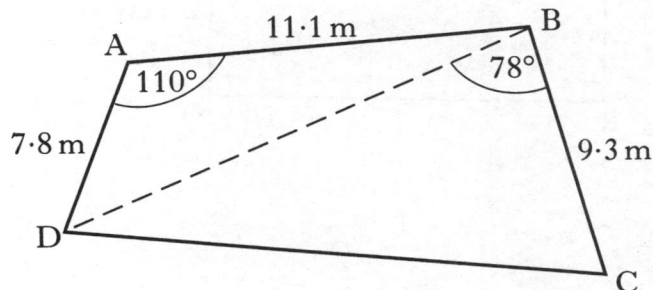

Calculate:

(a) the length of the diagonal BD;
Do not use a scale drawing   3

(b) the area of the garden.   4

[Turn over

8. The diagram shows an L-shaped metal plate.

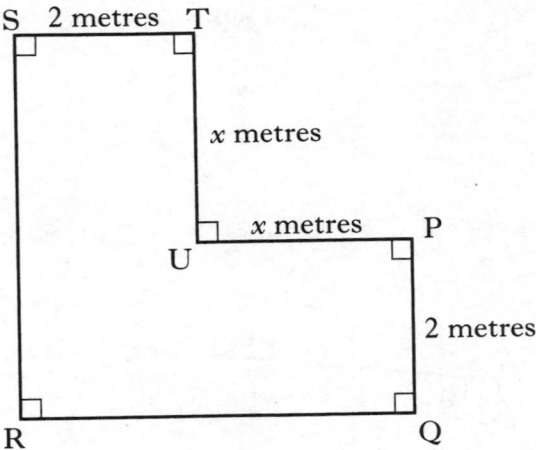

PQ = ST = 2 metres
TU = UP = x metres

(a) Show that the area, A square metres, of the metal plate is given by

$$A = 4x + 4.$$

(b) The area of the metal plate is 18 square metres.
Find x.

9. Perfecto Ice Cream is sold in cones and cylindrical tubs with measurements as shown below.

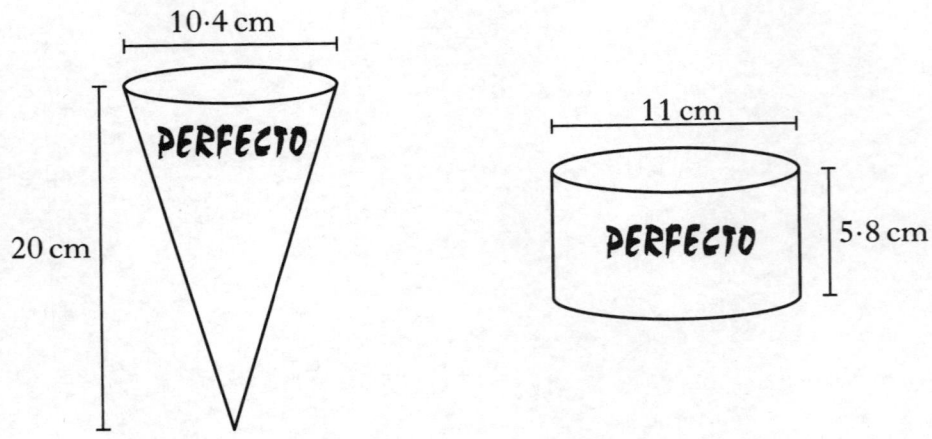

Both the cone and the tub of ice cream cost the same.
Which container of ice cream is better value for money?
Give a reason for your answer.

10. Solve the following equation for $0 \leq x \leq 360$.

$$7 \sin x° - 3 = 0$$

11. (a) Express $\dfrac{4}{x+3} + \dfrac{3}{x}$, $x \neq -3$, $x \neq 0$,

as a single fraction in its simplest form.

(b) Change the subject of the formula $m = \dfrac{3x + 2y}{p}$ to x.

(c) Simplify $\dfrac{3a^5 \times 2a}{a^2}$

[END OF QUESTION PAPER]

[BLANK PAGE]

2005 | Intermediate 2

X100/201

NATIONAL
QUALIFICATIONS
2005

FRIDAY, 20 MAY
1.00 PM – 1.45 PM

**MATHEMATICS
INTERMEDIATE 2**
Units 1, 2 and 3
Paper 1
(Non-calculator)

Read carefully

1 You may **NOT** use a calculator.

2 Full credit will be given only where the solution contains appropriate working.

3 Square-ruled paper is provided.

FORMULAE LIST

The roots of $ax^2 + bx + c = 0$ are $x = \dfrac{-b \pm \sqrt{(b^2 - 4ac)}}{2a}$

Sine rule: $\dfrac{a}{\sin A} = \dfrac{b}{\sin B} = \dfrac{c}{\sin C}$

Cosine rule: $a^2 = b^2 + c^2 - 2bc \cos A$ or $\cos A = \dfrac{b^2 + c^2 - a^2}{2bc}$

Area of a triangle: Area $= \tfrac{1}{2} ab \sin C$

Volume of a sphere: Volume $= \tfrac{4}{3}\pi r^3$

Volume of a cone: Volume $= \tfrac{1}{3}\pi r^2 h$

Volume of a cylinder: Volume $= \pi r^2 h$

Standard deviation: $s = \sqrt{\dfrac{\sum(x - \bar{x})^2}{n-1}} = \sqrt{\dfrac{\sum x^2 - (\sum x)^2 / n}{n-1}}$, where n is the sample size.

Official SQA Past Papers: Intermediate 2 Mathematics 2005

ALL questions should be attempted.

Marks

1. The stem and leaf diagram below shows the heights of a group of children.

   ```
   12 | 1  2  4  5  9
   13 | 0  0  1  5  7  8
   14 | 0  2  8  9
   15 | 1  1  2
   ```

   n = 18   12 | 1 represents 121 centimetres

   What is the probability that a child chosen at random from this group has a height less than 130 centimetres?   **1**

2.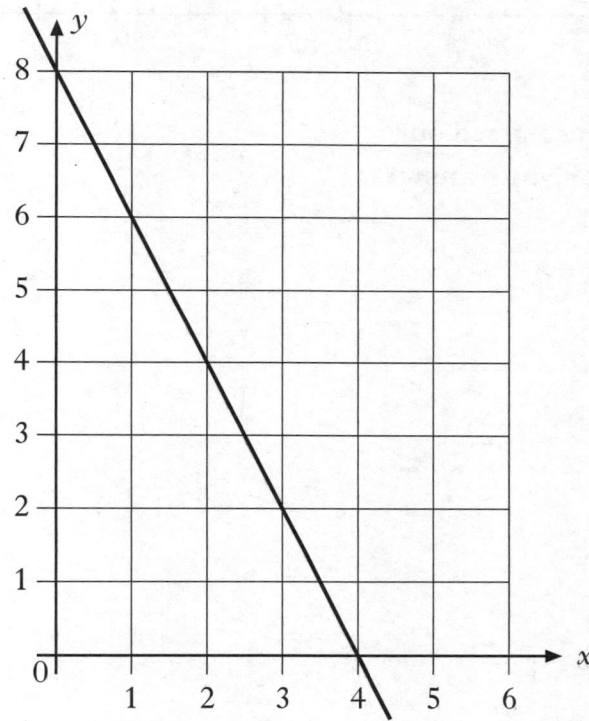

   (a) Find the equation of the straight line shown in the diagram.   **3**

   (b) Find the coordinates of the point where the line $y = 2x$ meets this line.   **2**

3. (a) Multiply out the brackets and collect like terms.

   $$(4x + 2)(x - 5) + 3x$$ **3**

   (b) Factorise

   $$2p^2 - 5p - 12.$$ **2**

[X100/201]   *Page three*   **[Turn over**

4. For a group of freezers in a shop, the volume, in litres, of each one is listed below.

$$78 \quad 81 \quad 91 \quad 75 \quad 85 \quad 83 \quad 84 \quad 78$$

(a) For the given data, calculate:
  (i) the median;
  (ii) the lower quartile;
  (iii) the upper quartile.

One of the numbers from the above list was accidentally missed out. A boxplot was then drawn and is shown below.

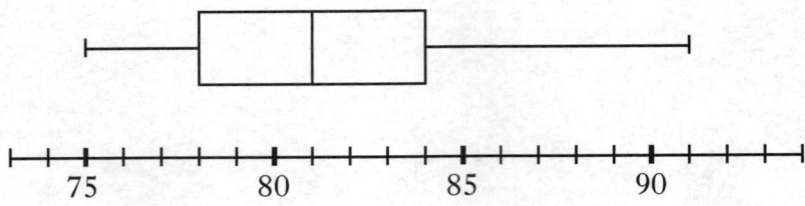

(b) Which number was missed out?
Give a reason for your answer.

5. Simplify

$$k^8 \times (k^2)^{-3}.$$

6. Given that

$$\tan 45° = 1,$$

what is the value of $\tan 135°$?

7. Sketch the graph of

$$y = \sin 2x°, \quad 0 \le x \le 360.$$

8. A rectangle has length $(x+2)$ centimetres and breadth x centimetres.

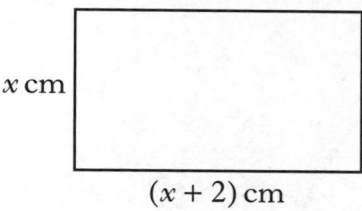

(a) Write down an expression for the area of the rectangle. **1**

A square has length $(x+1)$ centimetres.

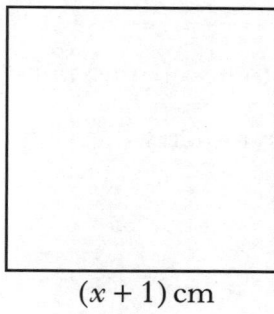

(b) The area of the square above is greater than the area of the rectangle. By how much is it greater? **2**

[Turn over for Question 9 on *Page six*

9. The diagram below shows part of the graph of $y = 36 - (x - 2)^2$.

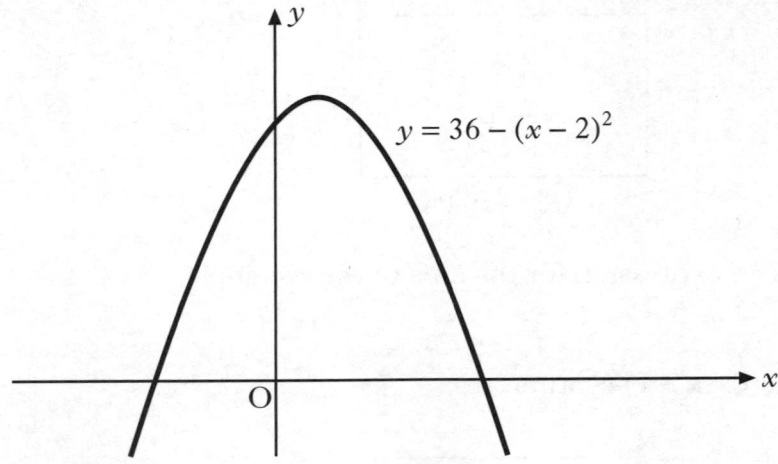

(a) State the coordinates of the maximum turning point.

(b) State the equation of the axis of symmetry.

The line $y = 20$ is drawn.
It cuts the graph of $y = 36 - (x - 2)^2$ at R and S as shown below.

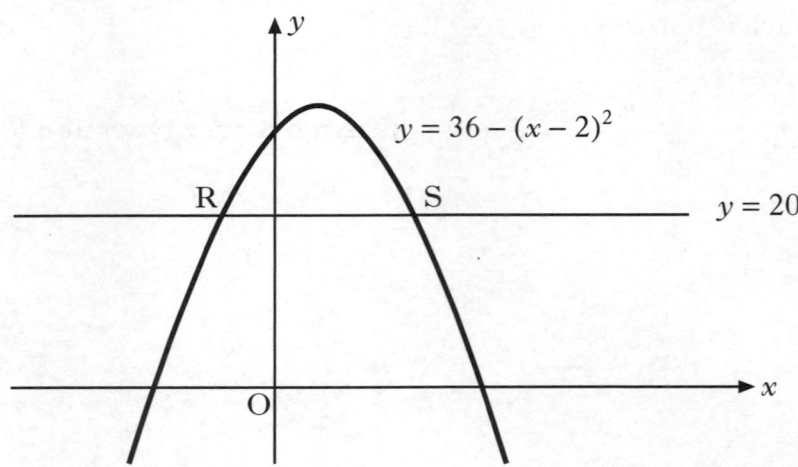

(c) S is the point (6, 20). Find the coordinates of R.

[END OF QUESTION PAPER]

Official SQA Past Papers: Intermediate 2 Mathematics 2005

X100/203

NATIONAL
QUALIFICATIONS
2005

FRIDAY, 20 MAY
2.05 PM – 3.35 PM

**MATHEMATICS
INTERMEDIATE 2
Units 1, 2 and 3
Paper 2**

Read carefully

1 **Calculators may be used in this paper.**

2 Full credit will be given only where the solution contains appropriate working.

3 Square-ruled paper is provided.

LIB X100/203 6/16370

FORMULAE LIST

The roots of $ax^2 + bx + c = 0$ are $x = \dfrac{-b \pm \sqrt{(b^2 - 4ac)}}{2a}$

Sine rule: $\dfrac{a}{\sin A} = \dfrac{b}{\sin B} = \dfrac{c}{\sin C}$

Cosine rule: $a^2 = b^2 + c^2 - 2bc \cos A$ or $\cos A = \dfrac{b^2 + c^2 - a^2}{2bc}$

Area of a triangle: Area $= \tfrac{1}{2} ab \sin C$

Volume of a sphere: Volume $= \tfrac{4}{3} \pi r^3$

Volume of a cone: Volume $= \tfrac{1}{3} \pi r^2 h$

Volume of a cylinder: Volume $= \pi r^2 h$

Standard deviation: $s = \sqrt{\dfrac{\sum(x - \bar{x})^2}{n-1}} = \sqrt{\dfrac{\sum x^2 - (\sum x)^2 / n}{n-1}}$, where n is the sample size.

ALL questions should be attempted.

1. In the evening, the temperature in a greenhouse drops by 4% per hour.
   At 8 pm the temperature is 28° Celsius.
   What will the temperature be at 11 pm?

2. In a bakery, a sample of six fruit loaves is selected and the weights, in grams, are recorded.

   395   400   408   390   405   402

   For the above data the mean is found to be 400 grams.

   (a) Calculate the standard deviation.

   Show clearly all your working.

   (b) New methods are introduced to ensure more consistent weights.

   Another sample is then taken and the mean and standard deviation found to be 400 grams and 5·8 grams respectively.

   Are the new methods successful?

   Give a reason for your answer.

3. A straight line has equation $3y = 12 - 4x$.
   Find the coordinates of the point where it crosses the x-axis.

[Turn over

Marks

4. A jeweller uses two different arrangements of beads and pearls.

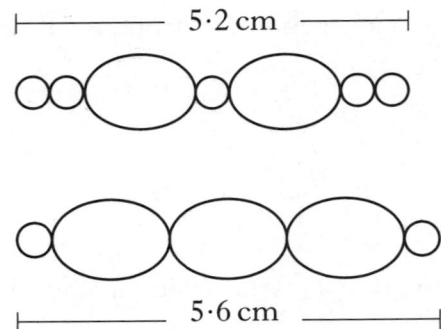

The first arrangement consists of 2 beads and 5 pearls and has an overall length of 5·2 centimetres.

The second arrangement consists of 3 beads and 2 pearls and has an overall length of 5·6 centimetres.

Find the length of **one** bead and the length of **one** pearl. 6

5. The diagram below shows a sector of a circle, centre C.

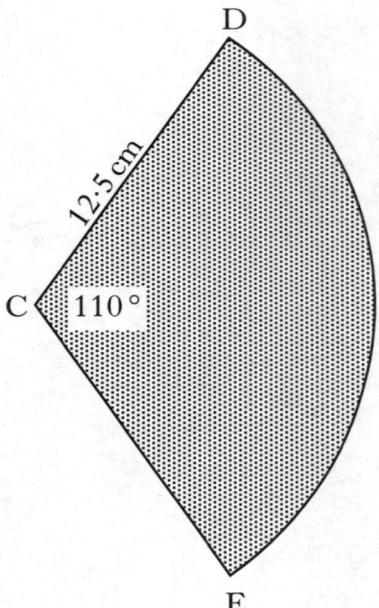

The radius of the circle is 12·5 centimetres and angle DCE is 110°.
Calculate the area of the sector CDE. 3

6. In the diagram below three towns, Holton, Kilter and Malbrigg are represented by the points H, K and M respectively.

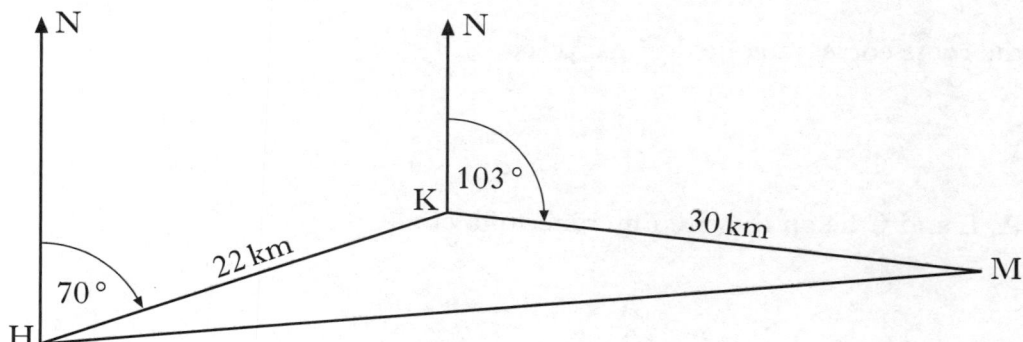

A helicopter flies from Holton for 22 kilometres on a bearing of 070° to Kilter. It then flies from Kilter for 30 kilometres on a bearing of 103° to Malbrigg. The helicopter then returns directly to Holton.

(a) (i) Calculate the size of angle HKM. **1**

(ii) Calculate the total distance travelled by the helicopter. **3**

Do not use a scale drawing.

(b) A climber is reported missing somewhere in the triangle represented by HKM in the diagram.

Calculate the area of this triangle. **2**

7. A pharmaceutical company makes vitamin pills in the shape of spheres of radius 0·5 centimetres.

(a) Calculate the volume of **one** pill.

Give your answer correct to two significant figures. **3**

The company decides to change the shape of each pill to a cylinder.

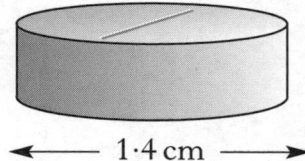

(b) The new pill has the **same** volume as the original and its diameter is 1·4 centimetres.

Calculate the height of the new pill. **3**

[Turn over

8. Solve the equation

$$4x^2 - 7x + 1 = 0$$

giving the roots correct to one decimal place. **4**

9. Points A, B and C lie on the circumference of a circle, centre O.

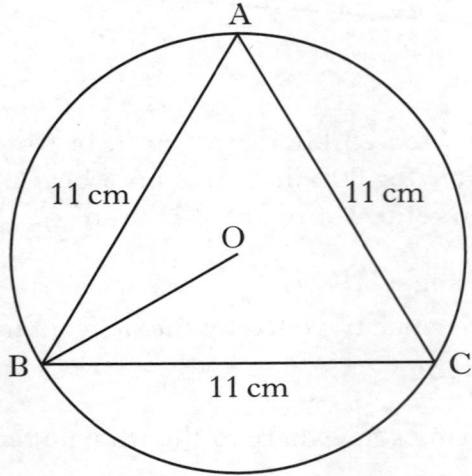

Triangle ABC is equilateral with sides of length 11 centimetres as shown in the diagram.

(a) Write down the size of angle OBC. **1**

(b) Calculate the length of the radius OB. **3**

Marks

10. (a) Express $\dfrac{7}{\sqrt{2}}$ as a fraction with a rational denominator.   2

(b) Express $\dfrac{a}{b} \times \dfrac{3b}{a^2}$ as a fraction in its simplest form.   2

(c) Change the subject of the formula

$$p = q + 2r^2 \quad \text{to } r.$$ 3

11. (a) Solve the equation

$$7 \cos x° - 5 = 0, \quad 0 \leq x < 360.$$ 3

(b) Simplify

$$\tan x° \cos x°.$$ 2

[END OF QUESTION PAPER]

[BLANK PAGE]

2006 | Intermediate 2

X100/201

NATIONAL
QUALIFICATIONS
2006

FRIDAY, 19 MAY
1.00 PM – 1.45 PM

**MATHEMATICS
INTERMEDIATE 2**
Units 1, 2 and 3
Paper 1
(Non-calculator)

Read carefully

1 You may **NOT** use a calculator.

2 Full credit will be given only where the solution contains appropriate working.

3 Square-ruled paper is provided.

FORMULAE LIST

The roots of $ax^2 + bx + c = 0$ are $x = \dfrac{-b \pm \sqrt{(b^2 - 4ac)}}{2a}$

Sine rule: $\dfrac{a}{\sin A} = \dfrac{b}{\sin B} = \dfrac{c}{\sin C}$

Cosine rule: $a^2 = b^2 + c^2 - 2bc \cos A$ or $\cos A = \dfrac{b^2 + c^2 - a^2}{2bc}$

Area of a triangle: Area $= \tfrac{1}{2} ab \sin C$

Volume of a sphere: Volume $= \tfrac{4}{3} \pi r^3$

Volume of a cone: Volume $= \tfrac{1}{3} \pi r^2 h$

Volume of a cylinder: Volume $= \pi r^2 h$

Standard deviation: $s = \sqrt{\dfrac{\sum(x - \bar{x})^2}{n - 1}} = \sqrt{\dfrac{\sum x^2 - (\sum x)^2 / n}{n - 1}}$, where n is the sample size.

ALL questions should be attempted.

1. The temperature, in degrees Celsius, at mid-day in a seaside town and the sales, in pounds, of umbrellas are shown in the scattergraph below.

   A line of best fit has been drawn.

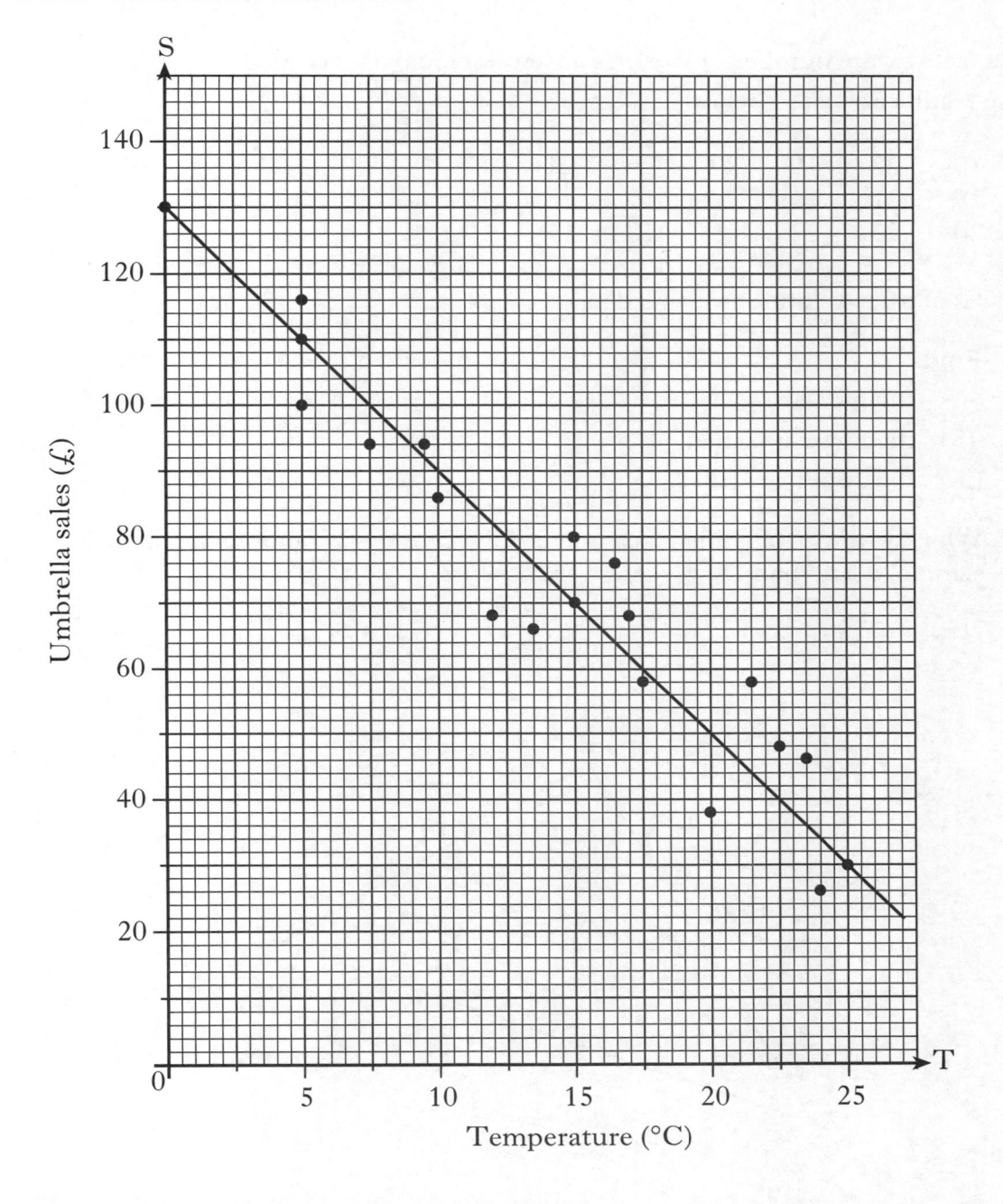

   (a) Find the equation of the line of best fit. 3

   (b) **Use your answer to part (a)** to predict the sales for a day when the temperature is 30 degrees Celsius. 1

[Turn over

Marks

2. Multiply out the brackets and collect like terms.

$$(2y - 3)(y^2 + 4y - 1)$$

3

3. In a factory, the number of workers absent each day is recorded for 21 days. The results are listed below.

19	22	19	22	20	21	17
19	21	16	20	19	18	18
20	20	23	19	18	17	19

   (a) Construct a dotplot for this data. 2

   (b) Find:
      (i) the median; 1
      (ii) the lower quartile; 1
      (iii) the upper quartile. 1

   (c) What is the probability that, on a day chosen at random from this sample, more than 18 workers were absent? 1

4.

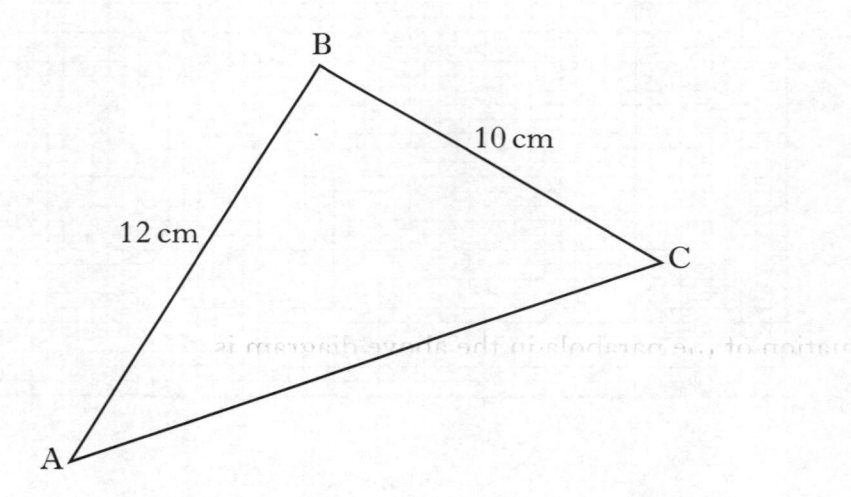

Calculate the area of triangle ABC if $\sin B = \frac{2}{3}$. 2

5. A straight line is represented by the equation $2y + x = 6$.

(a) Find the gradient of this line. **2**

(b) This line crosses the y-axis at $(0, c)$.
Find the value of c. **1**

6. Write the following in order of size, **starting with the smallest**.

$$\sin 0° \qquad \sin 30° \qquad \sin 200°$$

Give a reason for your answer. **2**

7.

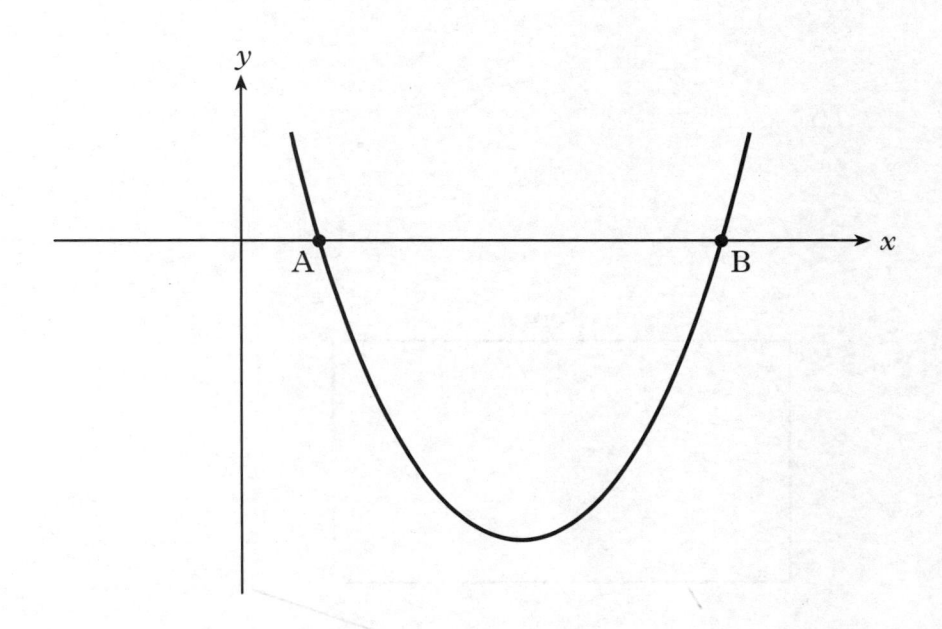

The equation of the parabola in the above diagram is

$$y = (x - 3)^2 - 4.$$

(a) State the coordinates of the minimum turning point of the parabola. **2**

(b) State the equation of the axis of symmetry of the parabola. **1**

(c) A is the point $(1, 0)$. State the coordinates of B. **1**

[Turn over for Questions 8 to 10 on *Page six*

8. The graph shown below has an equation of the form $y = \cos(x - a)°$.

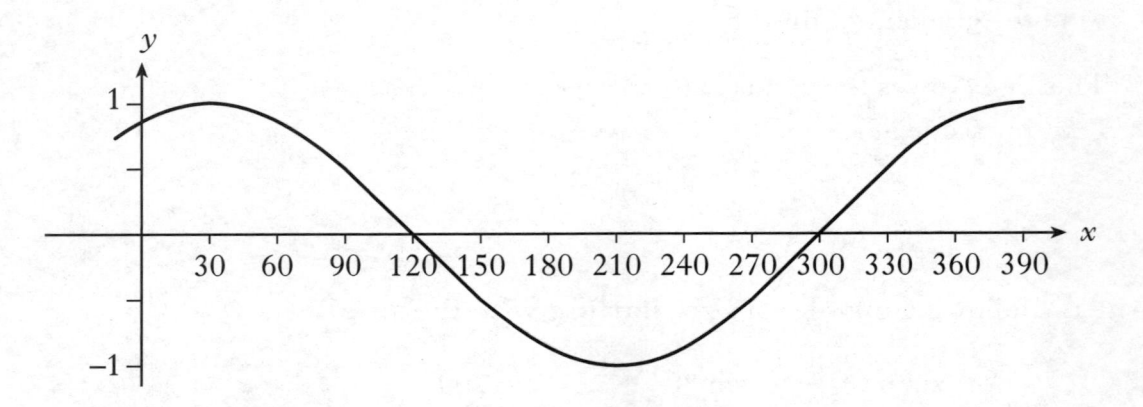

Write down the value of a.

9. Evaluate

$$16^{\frac{3}{4}}.$$

10.

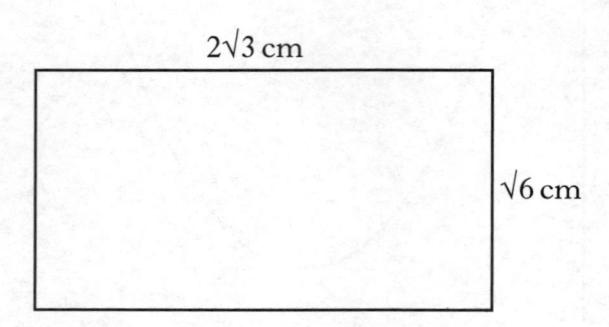

The rectangle above has length $2\sqrt{3}$ centimetres and breadth $\sqrt{6}$ centimetres.
Calculate the area of the rectangle.
Express your answer as a surd in its simplest form.

[END OF QUESTION PAPER]

X100/203

NATIONAL
QUALIFICATIONS
2006

FRIDAY, 19 MAY
2.05 PM – 3.35 PM

MATHEMATICS
INTERMEDIATE 2
Units 1, 2 and 3
Paper 2

Read carefully

1 **Calculators may be used in this paper.**

2 Full credit will be given only where the solution contains appropriate working.

3 Square-ruled paper is provided.

FORMULAE LIST

The roots of $ax^2 + bx + c = 0$ are $x = \dfrac{-b \pm \sqrt{(b^2 - 4ac)}}{2a}$

Sine rule: $\dfrac{a}{\sin A} = \dfrac{b}{\sin B} = \dfrac{c}{\sin C}$

Cosine rule: $a^2 = b^2 + c^2 - 2bc \cos A$ or $\cos A = \dfrac{b^2 + c^2 - a^2}{2bc}$

Area of a triangle: Area $= \tfrac{1}{2} ab \sin C$

Volume of a sphere: Volume $= \tfrac{4}{3}\pi r^3$

Volume of a cone: Volume $= \tfrac{1}{3}\pi r^2 h$

Volume of a cylinder: Volume $= \pi r^2 h$

Standard deviation: $s = \sqrt{\dfrac{\sum(x - \bar{x})^2}{n-1}} = \sqrt{\dfrac{\sum x^2 - (\sum x)^2 / n}{n-1}}$, where n is the sample size.

ALL questions should be attempted.

1. The value of a boat decreased from £35 000 to £32 200 in one year.

   (a) What was the percentage decrease?

   (b) If the value of the boat continued to fall at this rate, what would its value be after a **further** 3 years?
   Give your answer to the nearest hundred pounds.

2. Solve algebraically the system of equations

   $$4x + 2y = 13$$
   $$5x + 3y = 17.$$

3. A child's toy is in the shape of a hemisphere with a cone on top, as shown in the diagram.

   The toy is 10 centimetres wide and 16 centimetres high.

   Calculate the volume of the toy.

   Give your answer correct to 2 significant figures.

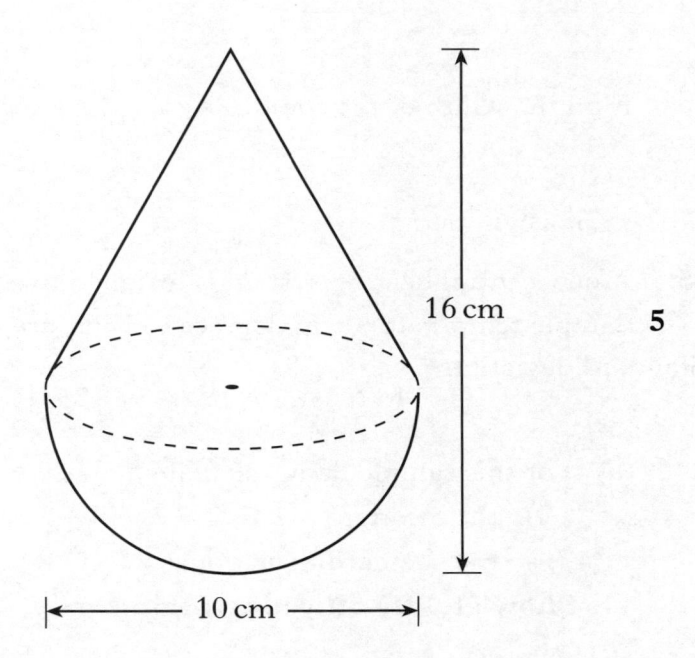

[Turn over

4. The diagram shows the base of a compact disc stand which has the shape of part of a circle.

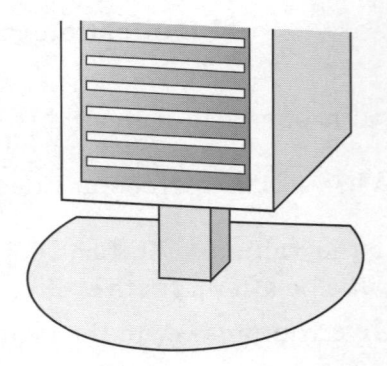

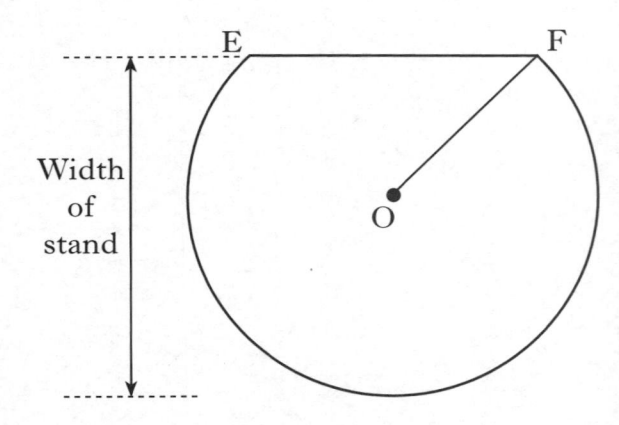

- The centre of the circle is O.
- EF is a chord of the circle.
- EF is 18 centimetres.
- The radius, OF, of the circle is 15 centimetres.

Find the width of the stand. **4**

5. A new central heating system is installed in a house.
Sample temperatures, in degrees Celsius, are recorded below.

$$19 \quad 21 \quad 23 \quad 21 \quad 19 \quad 20$$

(a) For this sample data, calculate:
   (i) the mean; **1**
   (ii) the standard deviation. **3**
   Show clearly all your working.

The target temperature for this house is 20 °Celsius. The system is judged to be operating effectively if the mean temperature is within 0·6 °Celsius of the target temperature **and** the standard deviation is less than 2 °Celsius.

(b) Is the system operating effectively?
   Give reasons for your answer. **2**

Marks

6. Factorise

$$4p^2 - 49.$$

2

7. Express

$$\frac{3}{(x+1)} - \frac{1}{(x-2)}, \quad x \neq -1, \quad x \neq 2$$

as a single fraction in its simplest form.

3

8. The diagram shows the penalty area in a football pitch.
All measurements are given in yards.

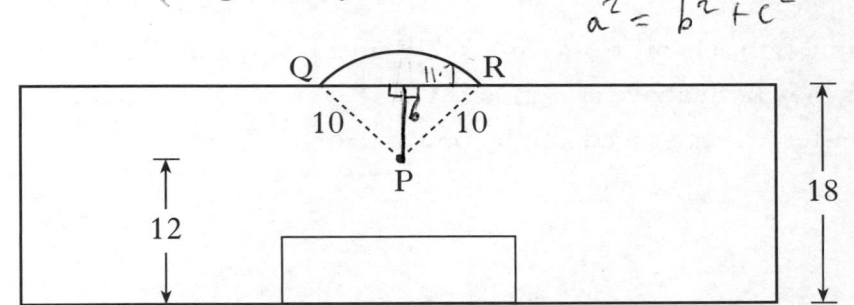

The penalty spot is marked at point P.
QR is an arc of a circle, centre P, radius 10 yards.
The width of the penalty area is 18 yards and the distance of the penalty spot from the goal line is 12 yards, as shown.

(a) Calculate the size of angle QPR.

3

(b) Calculate the length of arc QR.

2

9. Change the subject of the formula

$$\frac{x}{c} + a = b$$

to x.

2

[Turn over

10. The diagram below shows the position of three campsites A, B and C.

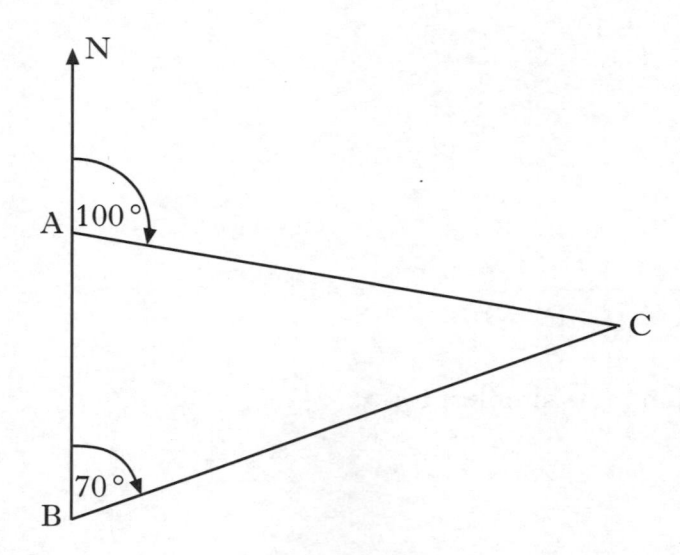

Alan sets off from campsite A on a bearing of 100° at an average speed of 5·6 kilometres per hour.

At the same time Bob sets off from campsite B on a bearing of 070°.

After 3 hours they both arrive at campsite C.

Who has the faster average speed and by how much? **5**

11. A cuboid is shown below.

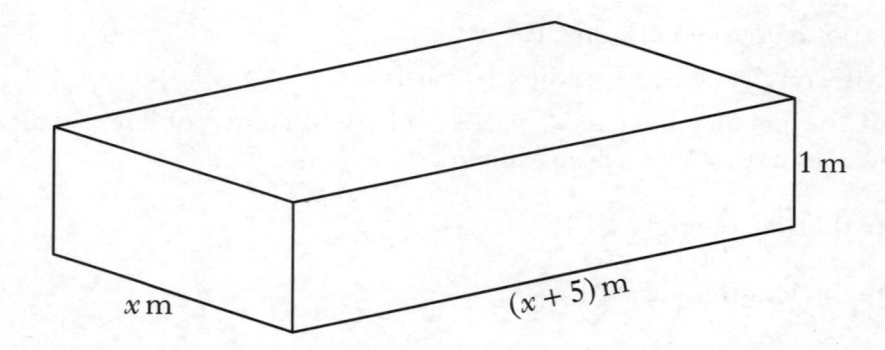

It has length $(x + 5)$ metres, breadth x metres, height 1 metre and volume 24 cubic metres.

(a) Show that

$$x^2 + 5x - 24 = 0.$$ **2**

(b) Using the equation in part (a), find the breadth of the cuboid. **3**

12. The arms on a wind turbine rotate at a steady rate.

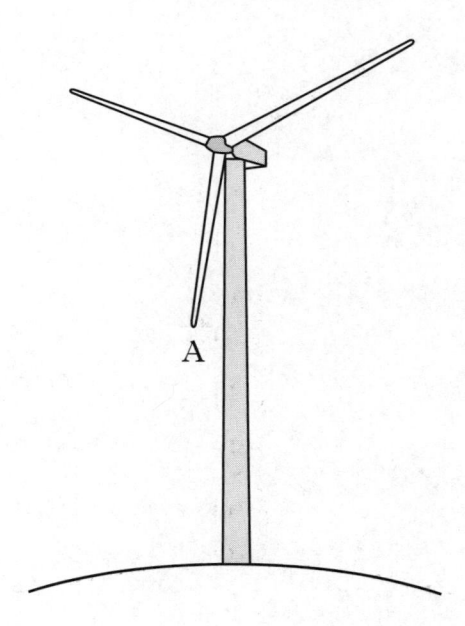

The height, h metres, of a point A above the ground at time t seconds is given by the equation

$$h = 8 + 4 \sin t°.$$

(a) Calculate the height of point A at time 30 seconds.

(b) Find the **two** times during the first turn of the arms when point A is at a height of 10·5 metres.

[END OF QUESTION PAPER]

[BLANK PAGE]

2007 | Intermediate 2

[BLANK PAGE]

X100/201

NATIONAL
QUALIFICATIONS
2007

TUESDAY, 15 MAY
1.00 PM – 1.45 PM

MATHEMATICS
INTERMEDIATE 2
Units 1, 2 and 3
Paper 1
(Non-calculator)

Read carefully

1 You may **NOT** use a calculator.

2 Full credit will be given only where the solution contains appropriate working.

3 Square-ruled paper is provided.

FORMULAE LIST

The roots of $ax^2 + bx + c = 0$ are $x = \dfrac{-b \pm \sqrt{(b^2 - 4ac)}}{2a}$

Sine rule: $\dfrac{a}{\sin A} = \dfrac{b}{\sin B} = \dfrac{c}{\sin C}$

Cosine rule: $a^2 = b^2 + c^2 - 2bc \cos A$ or $\cos A = \dfrac{b^2 + c^2 - a^2}{2bc}$

Area of a triangle: Area $= \tfrac{1}{2} ab \sin C$

Volume of a sphere: Volume $= \tfrac{4}{3} \pi r^3$

Volume of a cone: Volume $= \tfrac{1}{3} \pi r^2 h$

Volume of a cylinder: Volume $= \pi r^2 h$

Standard deviation: $s = \sqrt{\dfrac{\Sigma(x - \bar{x})^2}{n - 1}} = \sqrt{\dfrac{\Sigma x^2 - (\Sigma x)^2 / n}{n - 1}}$, where n is the sample size.

ALL questions should be attempted.

1. The table below shows the results of a survey of First Year pupils.

	Wearing a blazer	Not wearing a blazer
Boys	40	22
Girls	29	9

   What is the probability that a pupil, chosen at random from this sample, will be a girl wearing a blazer?

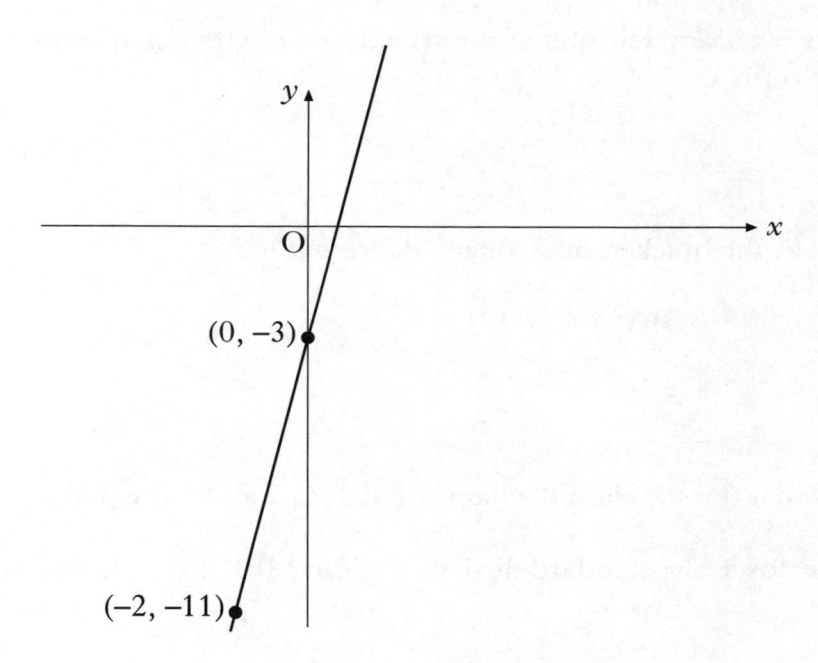

2. Find the equation of the straight line passing through the points $(0, -3)$ and $(-2, -11)$.

[Turn over

Marks

3. A tin of tuna is in the shape of a cylinder.

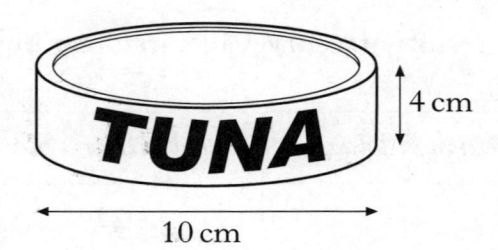

   It has diameter 10 centimetres and height 4 centimetres.
   Calculate its volume.
   Take $\pi = 3\cdot14$.   2

4. Find the point of intersection of the straight lines with equations $x + 2y = -5$ and $3x - y = 13$.   4

5. Multiply out the brackets and collect like terms.

   $$(x + 3)(x^2 + 4x - 12)$$ 3

6. (a) Show that the standard deviation of 1, 1, 1, 2 and 5 is equal to $\sqrt{3}$.   3

   (b) **Write down** the standard deviation of 101, 101, 101, 102 and 105.   1

7. The graph shown below is part of the parabola with equation $y = 8x - x^2$.

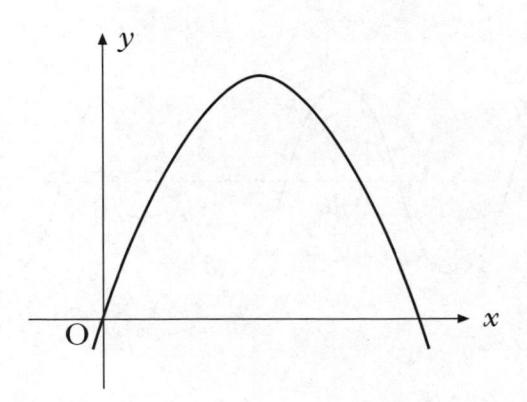

(a) By factorising $8x - x^2$, find the roots of the equation
$$8x - x^2 = 0.$$
2

(b) State the equation of the axis of symmetry of the parabola. **1**

(c) Find the coordinates of the turning point. **2**

8. Given that
$$\cos 60° = 0.5,$$
what is the value of $\cos 240°$? **1**

9. A right-angled triangle is shown below.

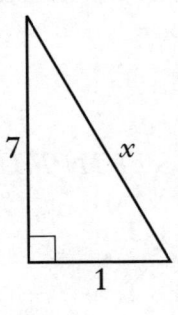

Using Pythagoras' Theorem, find x.
Express your answer as a surd in its simplest form. **3**

[Turn over for Questions 10 and 11 on *Page six*

10. (a) Part of the graph of $y = \cos ax°$ is shown below.

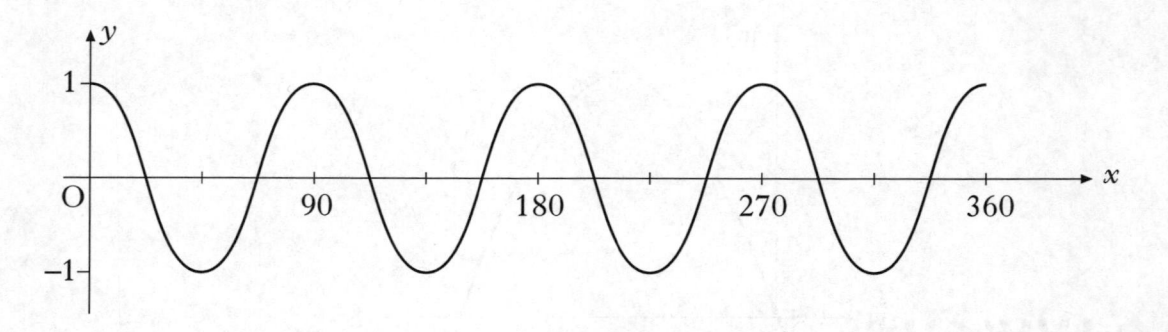

State the value of a.

(b) Part of the graph of $y = \tan bx°$ is shown below.

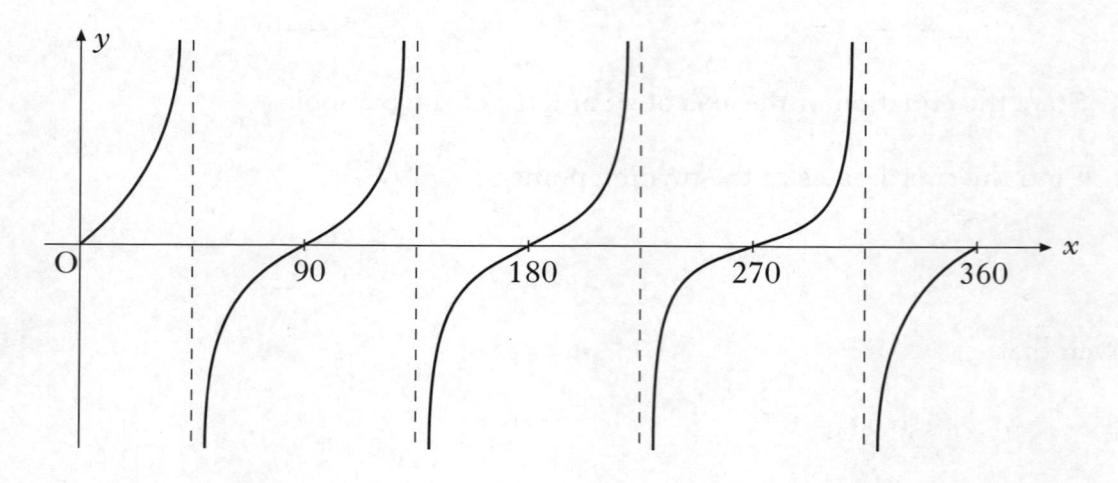

State the value of b.

11. A straight line is represented by the equation $y = ax + b$.

Sketch a possible straight line graph to illustrate this equation when $a = 0$ and $b > 0$.

[END OF QUESTION PAPER]

X100/203

NATIONAL
QUALIFICATIONS
2007

TUESDAY, 15 MAY
2.05 PM – 3.35 PM

MATHEMATICS
INTERMEDIATE 2
Units 1, 2 and 3
Paper 2

Read carefully

1 **Calculators may be used in this paper.**

2 Full credit will be given only where the solution contains appropriate working.

3 Square-ruled paper is provided.

FORMULAE LIST

The roots of $ax^2 + bx + c = 0$ are $x = \dfrac{-b \pm \sqrt{(b^2 - 4ac)}}{2a}$

Sine rule: $\dfrac{a}{\sin A} = \dfrac{b}{\sin B} = \dfrac{c}{\sin C}$

Cosine rule: $a^2 = b^2 + c^2 - 2bc \cos A$ or $\cos A = \dfrac{b^2 + c^2 - a^2}{2bc}$

Area of a triangle: Area $= \dfrac{1}{2} ab \sin C$

Volume of a sphere: Volume $= \dfrac{4}{3} \pi r^3$

Volume of a cone: Volume $= \dfrac{1}{3} \pi r^2 h$

Volume of a cylinder: Volume $= \pi r^2 h$

Standard deviation: $s = \sqrt{\dfrac{\Sigma(x - \bar{x})^2}{n - 1}} = \sqrt{\dfrac{\Sigma x^2 - (\Sigma x)^2 / n}{n - 1}}$, where n is the sample size.

ALL questions should be attempted.

Marks

1. Ian's annual salary is £28 400. His boss tells him that his salary will increase by 2·3% per annum.

   What will Ian's annual salary be after 3 years?

   Give your answer to the nearest pound. **3**

2. The diagram below shows a sector of a circle, centre C.

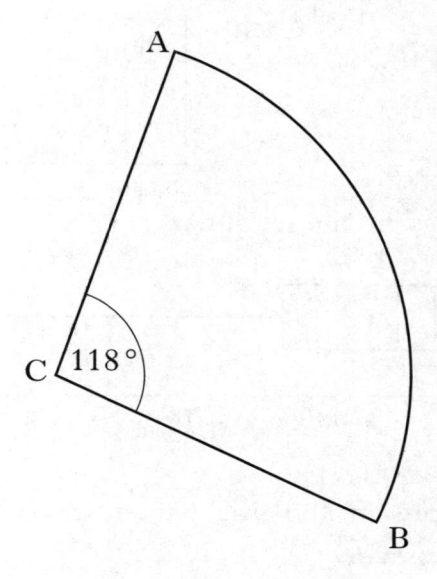

   The radius of the circle is 10·5 centimetres and angle ACB is 118°.
   Calculate the length of arc AB. **3**

   [Turn over

3. This back-to-back stem and leaf diagram shows the results for a class in a recent mathematics examination.

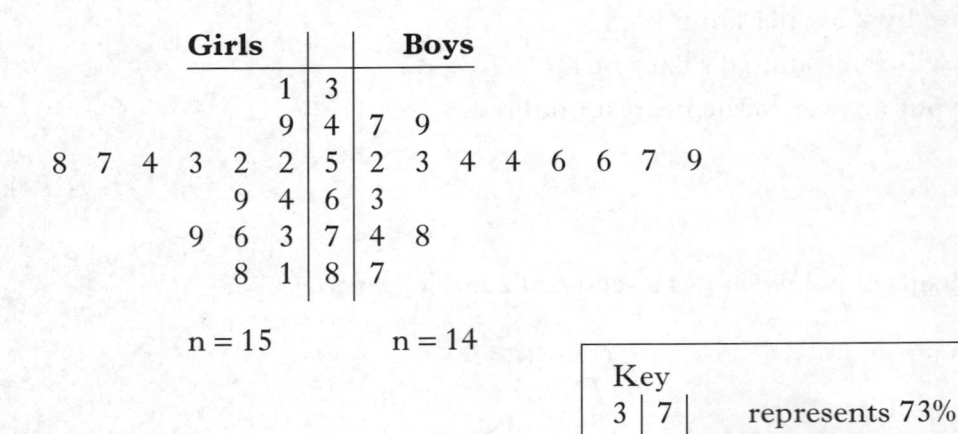

```
           Girls   |   | Boys
                 1 | 3 |
               9 | 4 | 7 9
   8 7 4 3 2 2 | 5 | 2 3 4 4 6 6 7 9
           9 4 | 6 | 3
         9 6 3 | 7 | 4 8
             8 1 | 8 | 7
```

n = 15   n = 14

Key
3 | 7 represents 73%
8 | 7 represents 87%

(a) A boxplot is drawn to represent one set of data.

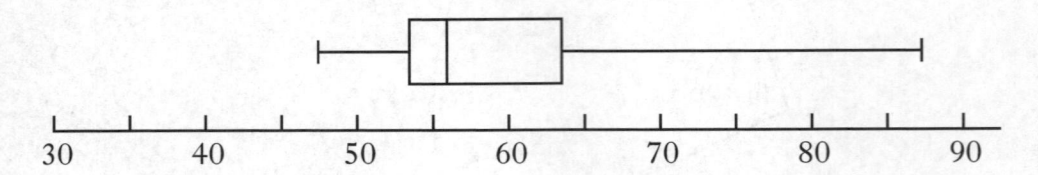

Does the boxplot above represent the girls' data or the boys' data?
Give a reason for your answer.   1

(b) For the **other** set of data, find:
  (i) the median;   1
  (ii) the lower quartile;   1
  (iii) the upper quartile.   1

(c) Use the answers found in part (b) to construct a second boxplot.   2

(d) Make an appropriate comment about the distribution of data in the two sets.   1

4.

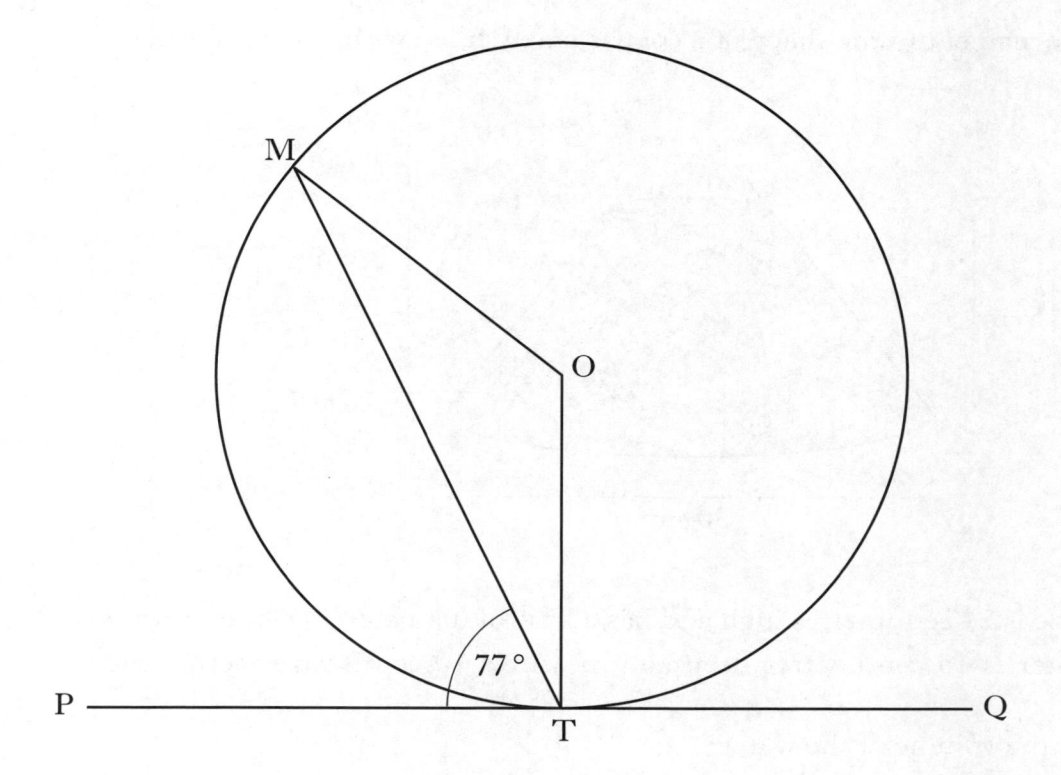

The tangent PQ touches the circle, centre O, at T.
Angle MTP is 77°.

(a) Calculate the size of angle MOT. **2**

(b) The radius of the circle is 8 centimetres.
Calculate the length of chord MT. **3**

[Turn over

5. A glass ornament in the shape of a cone is partly filled with coloured water.

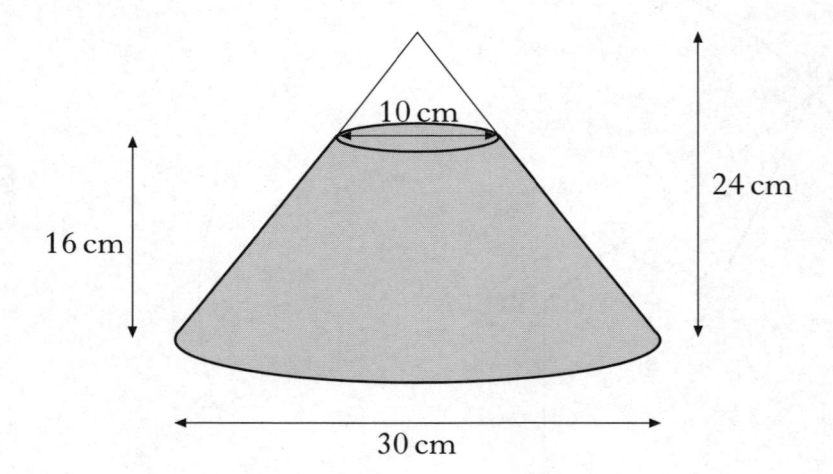

The cone is 24 centimetres high and has a base of diameter 30 centimetres.
The water is 16 centimetres deep and measures 10 centimetres across the top.
What is the volume of the water?
Give your answer correct to 2 significant figures. **5**

6. Tasnim rolls a standard dice with faces numbered 1 to 6.
The probability that she gets a number less than 7 is

    A 0
    B $\frac{1}{7}$
    C $\frac{1}{6}$
    D 1.

Write down the letter that corresponds to the correct probability. **1**

7. (a) Factorise **fully**
$$2x^2 - 18.$$
2

(b) Simplify
$$\frac{(2x+5)^2}{(2x-1)(2x+5)}$$
1

Marks

8. Solve the equation

$$2x^2 - 6x - 5 = 0,$$

giving the roots correct to one decimal place.

4

9. The diagram shows two blocks of flats of equal height.

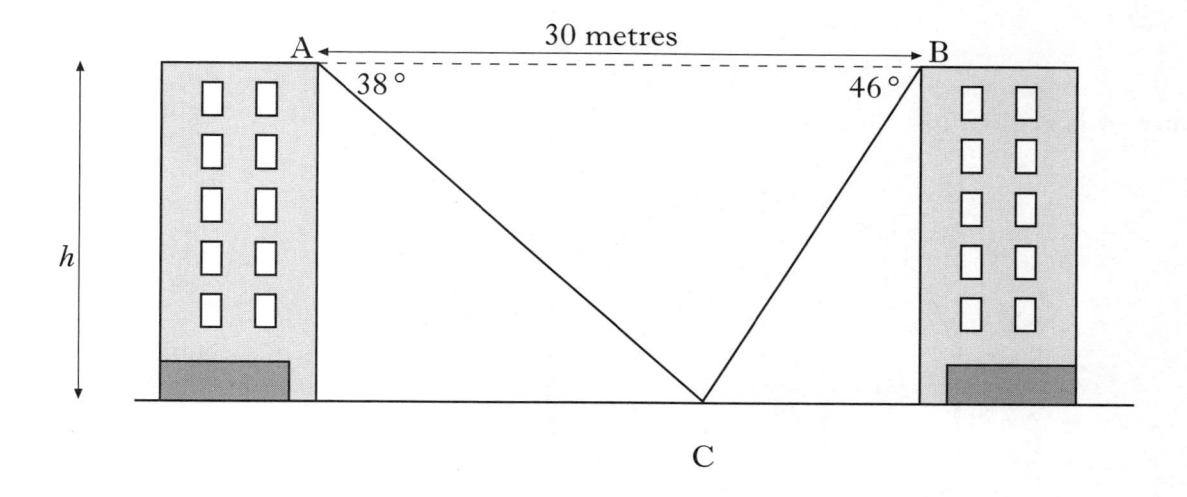

A and B represent points on the top of the flats and C represents a point on the ground between them.

To calculate the height, h, of each block of flats, a surveyor measures the angles of depression from A and B to C.

From A, the angle of depression is $38°$.
From B, the angle of depression is $46°$.
The distance AB is 30 metres.

Calculate the height, h, in metres.

5

10. Express $\dfrac{5p^2}{8} \div \dfrac{p}{2}$ as a fraction in its simplest form.

3

11. Change the subject of the formula

$$K = \dfrac{m^2 n}{p}$$

to m.

3

[Turn over for Questions 12, 13 and 14 on *Page eight*

Marks

12. Simplify the expression below, giving your answer with a positive power.

$$m^5 \times m^{-8}$$

2

13. Solve the equation

$$5 \tan x° - 6 = 2, \qquad 0 \leq x < 360.$$

3

14. A mirror is shaped like part of a circle.

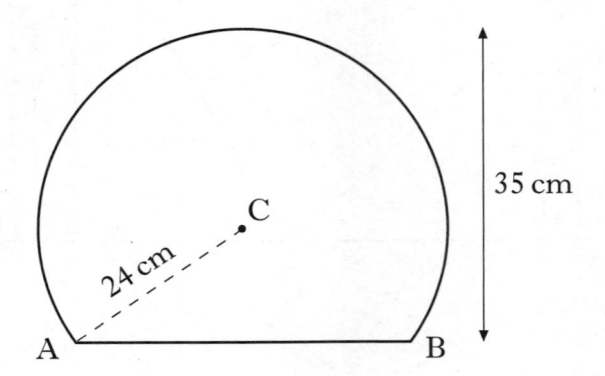

The radius of the circle, centre C, is 24 centimetres.
The height of the mirror is 35 centimetres.

Calculate the length of the base of the mirror, represented in the diagram by AB.

3

[END OF QUESTION PAPER]

2008 | Intermediate 2

X100/201

NATIONAL
QUALIFICATIONS
2008

TUESDAY, 20 MAY
1.00 PM – 1.45 PM

MATHEMATICS
INTERMEDIATE 2
Units 1, 2 and 3
Paper 1
(Non-calculator)

Read carefully

1 **You may NOT use a calculator.**

2 Full credit will be given only where the solution contains appropriate working.

3 Square-ruled paper is provided.

FORMULAE LIST

The roots of $ax^2 + bx + c = 0$ are $x = \dfrac{-b \pm \sqrt{(b^2 - 4ac)}}{2a}$

Sine rule: $\dfrac{a}{\sin A} = \dfrac{b}{\sin B} = \dfrac{c}{\sin C}$

Cosine rule: $a^2 = b^2 + c^2 - 2bc \cos A$ or $\cos A = \dfrac{b^2 + c^2 - a^2}{2bc}$

Area of a triangle: Area $= \tfrac{1}{2} ab \sin C$

Volume of a sphere: Volume $= \tfrac{4}{3} \pi r^3$

Volume of a cone: Volume $= \tfrac{1}{3} \pi r^2 h$

Volume of a cylinder: Volume $= \pi r^2 h$

Standard deviation: $s = \sqrt{\dfrac{\sum (x - \bar{x})^2}{n-1}} = \sqrt{\dfrac{\sum x^2 - (\sum x)^2 / n}{n-1}}$, where n is the sample size.

ALL questions should be attempted.

Marks

1. A straight line has equation $y = 4x + 5$.
   State the gradient of this line. **1**

2. Multiply out the brackets and collect like terms.

   $$(3x + 2)(x - 5) + 8x$$ **3**

3. The stem and leaf diagram shows the number of points gained by the football teams in the Premiership League in a season.

   ```
   3 | 3 3 3 9
   4 | 1 4 5 5 7 8
   5 | 0 2 3 3 6 6
   6 | 0
   7 | 5 9
   8 |
   9 | 0
   ```

   n = 20   4 | 1 represents 41 points

   (a) Arsenal finished 1st in the Premiership with 90 points.
   In what position did Southampton finish if they gained 47 points? **1**

   (b) What is the probability that a team chosen at random scored less than 44 points? **1**

4. (a) Factorise

   $$x^2 - y^2.$$ **1**

   (b) Hence, or otherwise, find the value of

   $$9 \cdot 3^2 - 0 \cdot 7^2.$$ **2**

   [Turn over

Marks

5. In a survey, the number of books carried by each girl in a group of students was recorded.

   The results are shown in the frequency table below.

Number of books	Frequency
0	1
1	2
2	3
3	5
4	5
5	6
6	2
7	1

   (a) Copy this frequency table and add a cumulative frequency column.   1

   (b) For this data, find:
      (i) the median;   1
      (ii) the lower quartile;   1
      (iii) the upper quartile.   1

   (c) Calculate the semi-interquartile range.   1

   (d) In the same survey, the number of books carried by each boy was also recorded.

   The semi-interquartile range was 0·75.

   Make an appropriate comment comparing the distribution of data for the girls and the boys.   1

6. Triangle PQR is shown below.

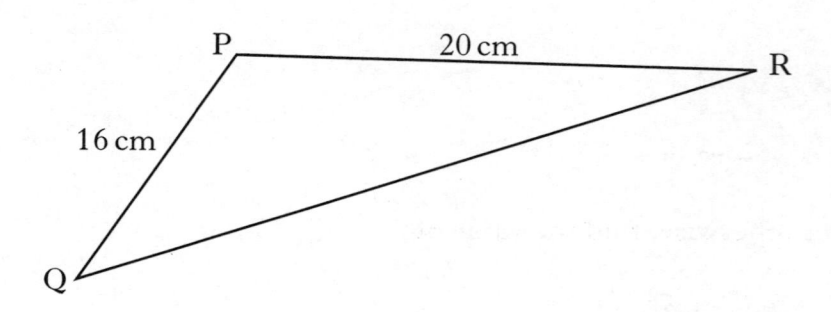

   P to R = 20 cm, P to Q = 16 cm.

   If $\sin P = \frac{1}{4}$, calculate the area of triangle PQR.   2

[X100/201]   *Page four*

7.

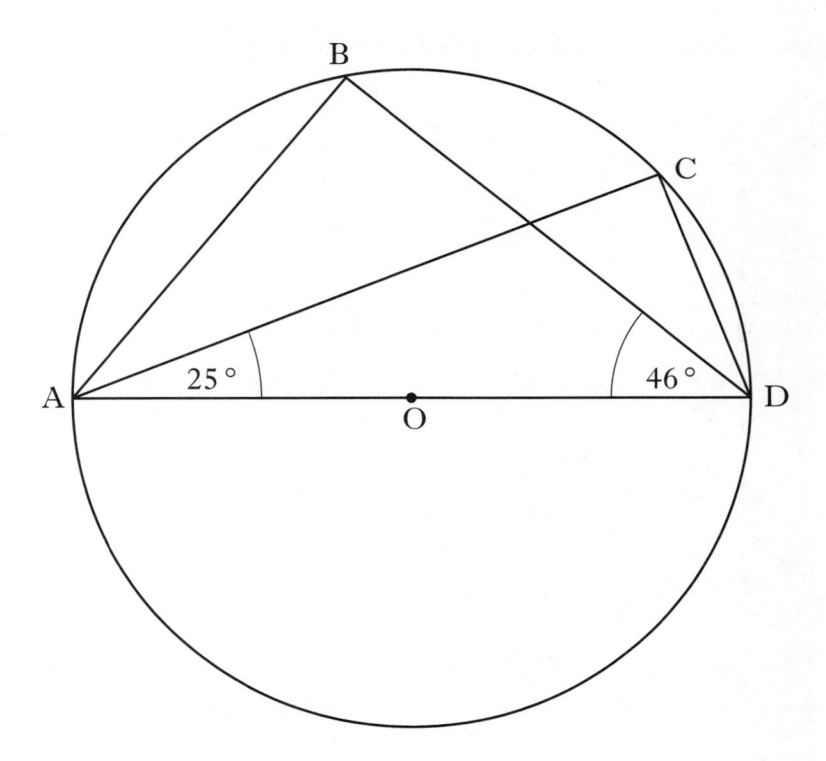

AD is a diameter of a circle, centre O.
B and C are points on the circumference of the circle.
Angle CAD = 25°.
Angle BDA = 46°.
Calculate the size of angle BAC. **3**

8. Part of the graph of $y = a \sin bx°$ is shown in the diagram.

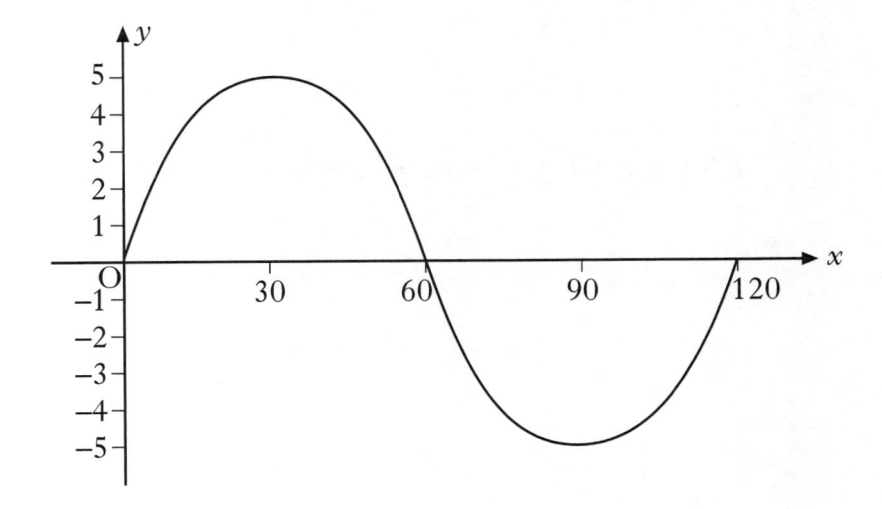

State the values of a and b. **2**

[Turn over for Questions 9 and 10 on *Page six*

9. The graph below shows part of a parabola with equation of the form

$$y = (x + a)^2 + b.$$

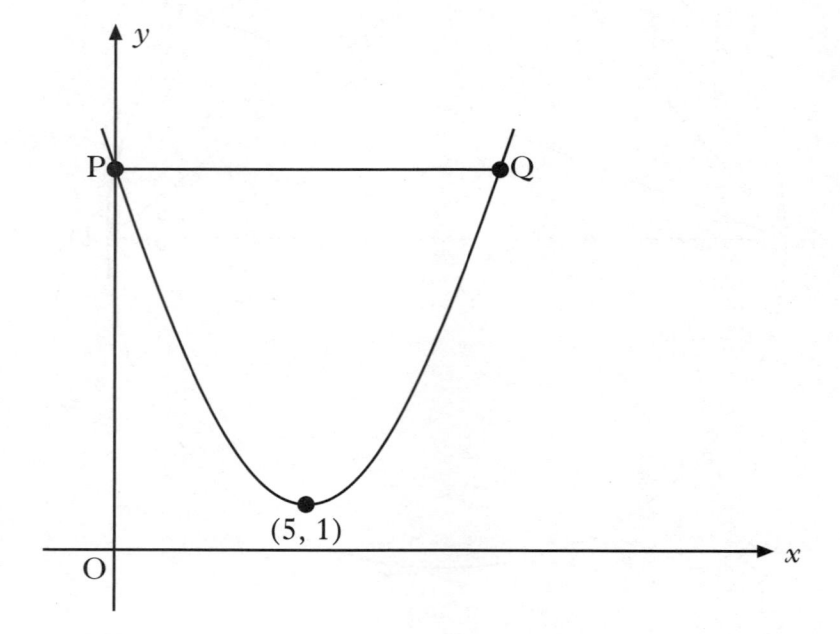

(5, 1)

(a) State the values of a and b. **2**

(b) State the equation of the axis of symmetry of the parabola. **1**

(c) The line PQ is parallel to the x-axis.
Find the coordinates of points P and Q. **3**

10. If $\sin x° = \dfrac{4}{5}$ and $\cos x° = \dfrac{3}{5}$, calculate the value of $\tan x°$. **2**

[END OF QUESTION PAPER]

X100/203

NATIONAL
QUALIFICATIONS
2008

TUESDAY, 20 MAY
2.05 PM – 3.35 PM

**MATHEMATICS
INTERMEDIATE 2
Units 1, 2 and 3
Paper 2**

Read carefully

1 **Calculators may be used in this paper.**

2 Full credit will be given only where the solution contains appropriate working.

3 Square-ruled paper is provided.

FORMULAE LIST

The roots of $ax^2 + bx + c = 0$ are $x = \dfrac{-b \pm \sqrt{(b^2 - 4ac)}}{2a}$

Sine rule: $\dfrac{a}{\sin A} = \dfrac{b}{\sin B} = \dfrac{c}{\sin C}$

Cosine rule: $a^2 = b^2 + c^2 - 2bc \cos A$ or $\cos A = \dfrac{b^2 + c^2 - a^2}{2bc}$

Area of a triangle: Area $= \tfrac{1}{2} ab \sin C$

Volume of a sphere: Volume $= \tfrac{4}{3} \pi r^3$

Volume of a cone: Volume $= \tfrac{1}{3} \pi r^2 h$

Volume of a cylinder: Volume $= \pi r^2 h$

Standard deviation: $s = \sqrt{\dfrac{\sum (x - \bar{x})^2}{n-1}} = \sqrt{\dfrac{\sum x^2 - (\sum x)^2 / n}{n-1}}$, where n is the sample size.

ALL questions should be attempted.

Marks

1. Calculate the **compound interest** earned when £50 000 is invested for 4 years at 4·5% per annum.

   Give your answer to the nearest penny.   4

2. Jim Reid keeps his washing in a basket. The basket is in the shape of a prism.

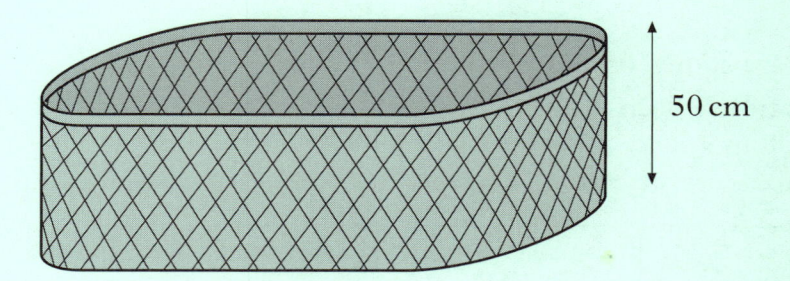

   The height of the basket is 50 centimetres.

   The cross section of the basket consists of a rectangle and two semi-circles with measurements as shown.

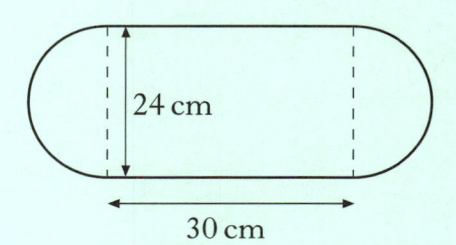

   (a) Find the volume of the basket in cubic centimetres.

   Give your answer correct to three significant figures.   4

   Jim keeps his ironing in a storage box which has a volume **half** that of the basket.

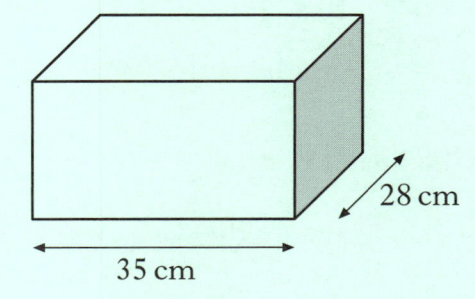

   The storage box is in the shape of a cuboid, 35 centimetres long and 28 centimetres broad.

   (b) Find the height of the storage box.   3

3. The results for a group of students who sat tests in mathematics and physics are shown below.

Mathematics (%)	10	18	26	32	49
Physics (%)	25	35	30	40	41

(a) Calculate the standard deviation for the mathematics test.   4

(b) The standard deviation for physics was 6·8.
Make an appropriate comment on the distribution of marks in the two tests.   1

These marks are shown on the scattergraph below.
A line of best fit has been drawn.

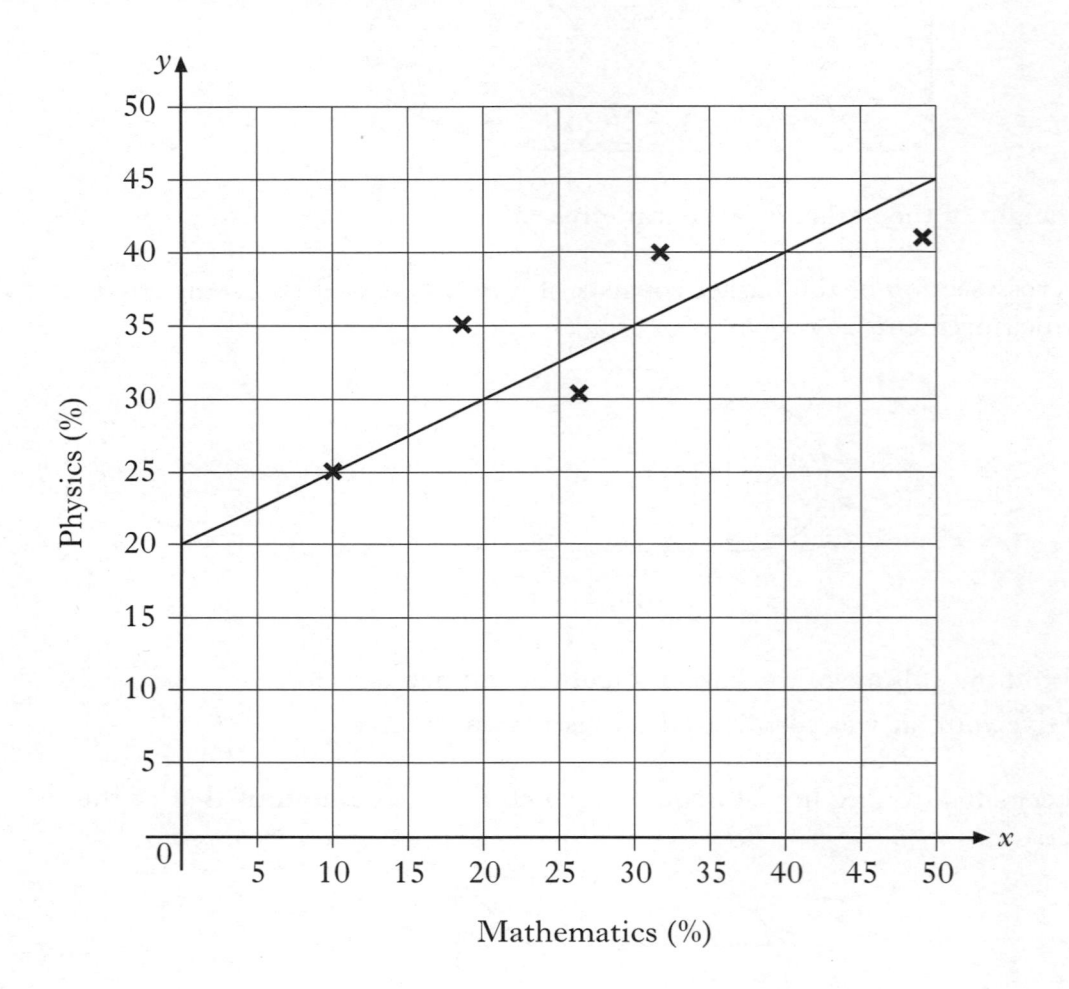

(c) Find the equation of the line of best fit.   3

(d) Another pupil scored 76% in the mathematics test but was absent from the physics test.
Use your answer to part (c) to predict his physics mark.   1

Marks

4. Suzie has a new mobile phone. She is charged x pence per minute for calls and y pence for each text she sends. During the first month her calls last a total of 280 minutes and she sends 70 texts. Her bill is £52·50.

    (a) Write down an equation in x and y which satisfies the above condition. **1**

    The next month she reduces her bill. She restricts her calls to 210 minutes and sends 40 texts. Her bill is £38·00.

    (b) Write down a second equation in x and y which satisfies this condition. **1**

    (c) Calculate the price per minute for a call and the price for each text sent. **4**

5. Triangle DEF is shown below.

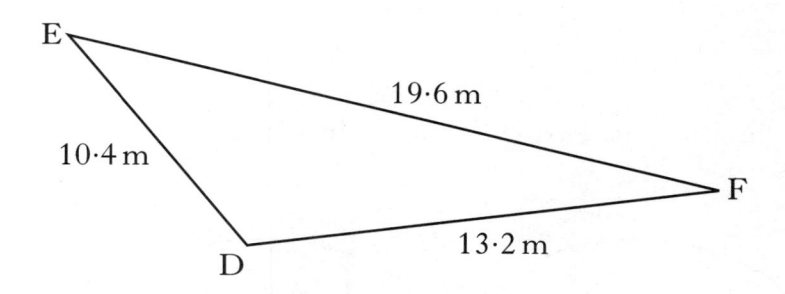

    It has sides of length 10·4 metres, 13·2 metres and 19·6 metres.
    Calculate the size of angle EDF.
    Do not use a scale drawing. **3**

6. Solve the equation

    $$5x^2 + 4x - 2 = 0,$$

    giving the roots correct to 2 decimal places. **4**

[Turn over

7. (a) Simplify

$$\frac{m^5}{m^3}.$$

(b) Express

$$2\sqrt{5} + \sqrt{20} - \sqrt{45}$$

as a surd in its simplest form.

8. Solve the equation

$$4\cos x° + 3 = 0, \quad 0 \le x \le 360.$$

9. Two identical circles, with centres P and Q, intersect at A and B as shown in the diagram.

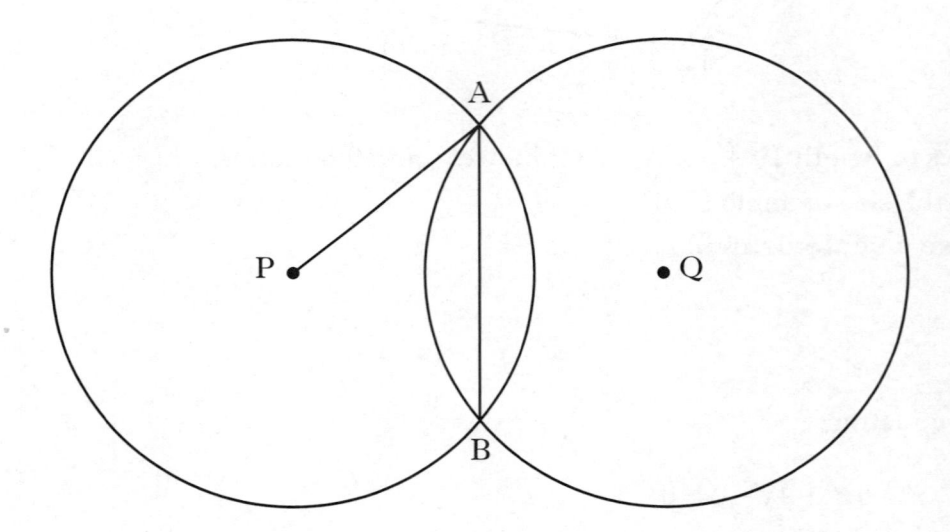

The radius of each circle is 10 centimetres.
The length of the common chord, AB, is 12 centimetres.

Calculate PQ, the distance between the centres of the two circles.

10. Change the subject of the formula

$$p = q + \sqrt{a}$$

to a.

11. Express

$$\frac{2}{a} - \frac{3}{(a+4)}, \quad a \neq 0, \ a \neq -4,$$

as a single fraction in its simplest form.

[END OF QUESTION PAPER]

[BLANK PAGE]

[BLANK PAGE]

[BLANK PAGE]

[BLANK PAGE]